Complete with step-by-step strategies and practical information for every sail or power boater

- Store **emergency information** and procedures—so you **know what to do** when you have a problem

- Set up a **"to do" list** and **boat organizer**—don't overlook important equipment or repairs before you go out on the water

- Keep a **record** of repairs, suppliers—**money!**

- **Organize** and **speed up** your outfitting and maintenance—get more time on the water

- Create a pleasure **boating journal**—keep those wonderful (and sometimes exciting) cruising memories alive

In one handy book, here is everything you want to use, keep, remember, organize or record about your boat and your boating activities

Boat Information

Boat Name:

License Registration:

Type of Vessel:

Slip or buoy number:

Location

Home Port:

State of Registry:

Owner Name:

Telephone Numbers: Home (   )   Business (   )

Mailing address: Street

City   State   Zip

Where I might also be reached:

BOAT BOOK compiled by:

Date book begun:

REWARD OFFERED: *In case this book is lost, please call me at the above telephone number or return it to me at the above address. Thank you.*

✭ ✭ ✭ ✭ ✭ ✭

MarLor's
BOAT BOOK

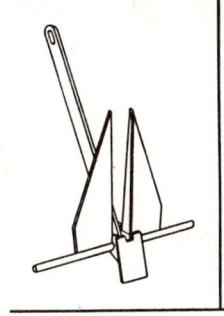

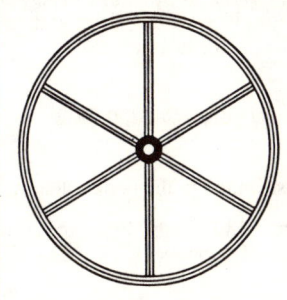

With special forward
by Marlin Bree

ML
—
MARLOR PRESS

Copyright 1989

by MARLIN BREE

MARLOR'S BOAT BOOK. Published by MarLor Press. All rights reserved. No part of this book may be reproduced in any form without the written permission of MarLor Press

ISBN 0-943400-39-2

Distributed to the book trade by:

Contemporary Books Inc./ 180 North Michigan Avenue/ Chicago, Illinois 60601/ Telephone/ (312) 782-9181

First Edition: September 1989

ML

MARLOR PRESS

4304 Brigadoon Drive/ Saint Paul, MN 55126/ Telephone (612) 484-4600

Contents

Section 1 / ABOUT THIS BOOK

Boat emergency directory, **8**
Special forward, **9**
How to use this book, **11**

Section 2 / BOAT ORGANIZER

Getting organized for better boating

My boat basic specifications & data, **18**
Boat equipment record, **20**
Major suppliers: Names, addresses & telephones, **22**
To do lists, **24**
Purchasing organizer & record, **26**
Workbook, **28**

Section 3 / CRUISE ORGANIZER

Better procedures for more and better time on the water

Getting ready to go, **32**
Chores: Before & after, **34**
Crew members, **36**
Crew duties, **39**
Watch schedules, **41**
Welcome aboard! Guest embarking suggestions, **42**

Section 4 / BOATING JOURNAL

Keeping the information you want to remember

50-cruise structured recreational boating journal, **44**
 Time/ sea state/ weather/ destination/ & cruising information
Future cruises & ideas, **94**

Section 5 / GETTING SHIPSHAPE

With checklists and action schedules

Spring commissioning checklist, **96**
Spring action list, **100**
Fall layup and storage checklist, **102**
Fall action list, **104**

Section 6 / EMERGENCY

Captain's emergency instructions:

Man overboard instructions, **108**

VHF radio emergency calls, **109**

Fire, **111**

Hull taking on water, **112**

Section 7 / RECORDS, SYSTEMS & COSTS

Galley basics, **114**
Boat supplies, **116**
Chart locker, **118**
Rope locker & record, **120**
Boat gear locator, **121**
Names, addresses and telephone numbers, **122**
Expenditures, **124**
Appointments & schedules, **126**

Section 1

Boat emergency directory

Special forward

How to use this book

Boat emergency directory

By order of and filled out by

Captain

MAN OVERBOARD instructions, see page **108**

EMERGENCY VHF radio call, see page **109**

FIRE, see page **111**

HULL TAKING ON WATER, see page **112**

EMERGENCY TELEPHONE NUMBERS:

Police:

Fire department:

Coast Guard:

Medical emergency numbers:

Insurance agent telephones:
  Office   Home

Company insured with:
  Address
  City   State   Zip
  Telephone Numbers

Policy Number: **Expiration:**

Coverage limits:

Marina telephone: **Boat mechanic:**

Special Foreword

THIS IS A BOOK I've always wanted to have. Like many other boaters, I carried things around in my mind that I wanted to remember to do (often forgetting them). Or I had papers with things written on them stuffed in my working jeans—and still other tablets with more writing in my boat's workshop. More were on board my boat. These papers and tablets contained my "to do" lists, items of equipment or supplies I needed to buy, names and telephone numbers of suppliers or fellow boaters, and even things to do to prepare my boat for spring launching or fall layup.

Trouble is, I sometimes misplace a number of these papers. I can always count on having at least one important paper or tablet in the wrong place. So I easily can see the need for the **Boat Book**, which organizes any boater's want-to-do, have-to-do information into one central source.

It's a working book for anyone who putters about or actively sails a pleasure boat. This **Boat Book** can be used by both beginners or more experienced boaters. It can be used a lot—or, for that matter, a little. And best of all, a little bit at a time.

What's important is that this book is at last that handy place where boaters can have a central source for mastery of their vessels' details as well as record some of their delight and interest in it. This organizer ranges in scope from keeping basic mechanical data about the boat and its equipment, such as the type of spark plugs and gap your engine uses, to information to systematize the hassle of the once-a-year-routine of commissioning the boat for another season. Or, keeping track of on-board equipment and registration numbers, for warranty or insurance purposes.

It's handy and easily transportable—so sailors can carry it around in a jacket pocket. Or, leave it on their boat's worktable. Or put on the deck as they work on a project, jotting down details, or take with them as they purchase items at their ship's store. Or tote it back to the office to keep handy to arrange for mail order marine purchases.

If boaters work with this book in the spirit it's intended, often just a few minutes at a time, they'll find it soon will be packed with useful information that will help them not only understand their boat more—but get more enjoyment from their time on the water.

Because boats can be quite complex in their operation and maintenance, you'll want to become familiar with these pages as well as the information that is to be recorded. Be fairly conscientious about the detail—and you'll find that your **Boat Book** is the place to turn to make a decision about your boat.

The best part about keeping a book like this is that it will be not only a record of your facts and planning, but also of your thoughts and feelings.

After all, this book is about you, your boat, your crew and friends and your adventures together on the water. You'll quickly find it also will be a voyage to self-discovery. As you write in your **Boat Book**, you'll probably get useful new tacks on the way you look at things and make decisions. Self-discovery is a basic step to becoming a better sailor.

When you're not working with your **Boat Book**, you can keep it on a shelf for handy reference. Since it is your writing about your own vessel and your experiences together, you and your crew will find it to be a fascinating record. Its's **your** history, after all.

Marlin Bree

Marlin Bree is the author of *In the Teeth of the Northeaster:* A solo voyage on Lake Superior, and is the co-author with Gerry Spiess of the national best-selling book, *Alone Against the Atlantic.* Bree's writings also have appeared in boating magazines and he is on the book review staff of one national sailing magazine .

How to use this book

THIS IS A WORKING BOOK for your use. If you take just a few minutes a day, you can soon develop this book to be an outstanding resource for you and your crew's use—as well as a terrific way to store your information and memories.

Section 1 / ABOUT THIS BOOK

The beginning section contains the **index** for your vessel's **Emergency Directory**. Be certain to fill out the useful telephone numbers and information—as well as the **Emergency Directory** beginning on page 108.

Section 2 / BOAT ORGANIZER

This section contains the **Basic Specifications** of your boat. Here you record basic data about your boat, such as its length, width, displacement, freeboard and draft.

Also in this section is your **Boating Equipment Record.** Here is the place for you to keep the details of your major pieces of equipment as well as serial numbers. Over the years, it's surprising how useful this record can be when replacing equipment or performing maintenance. **Serial numbers** are needed if, for example, a piece of equipment, such as your spare outboard, is missing and you need to identify it.

It's a good idea to make a machine copy of this **Record** and keep it somewhere safe.. It's also useful to have a single-source record of your **Major Suppliers** so that, for example, if an instrument fails on a cruise, you'll know who to call and what to ask for.

Your **Purchasing Organizer and Record** is useful for those items you want to purchase the next time your visit your marine store or supplier or send off for materials. Think of it as your boat's *shopping list*. Use it to write down things as you think of them. **Your "to do" list** is where you write down projects you *want to do*. This can range from touching up some of the forward brightwork to noting that the next time you pull your boat it's time to check your knotmeter's paddlewheel.

Your **Workbook** can be a fascinating part of your **Boat Book**. If you're handy with tools, this is where you can write down, sketch, and develop some of the ideas you want for your boat. A mahogany or teak item for your boat? A new shelf for your navigator's station? Or a bookshelf above a bunk? Here is a section for **your ideas**. The first step to making a project a reality is to write it down.

Boating is a sport, an adventure, a leisure activity. But above all, it's a happy, endless cycle of dreaming, creating, then enjoying. So don't be afraid to be adventurous with your boat or hesitate to begin some new creations on board that will add to your fun or safety aboard your vessel. Remember that good boats are like good friends and spouses: *they don't get older—they get better!*

Section 3 / CRUISE ORGANIZER

If you've ever gotten underway and suddenly realized you'd forgotten something important back on shore, then you know how important it is to write down some of the information you've tended to carry around in your head. This section is a way to keep detailed information in a handy place for easy and routine reference. As in other sections of this book, you can do as little, or as much, as you see fit—do whatever suits your nautical temperament.

A **Getting Ready to Go** list details what you want to remember as you get ready to take your vessel away from the dock—a busy time. This is your own checklist for your own use. It can remind you, for example, to check to see that the tanks are topped up. Or to run the blower in the engine compartment prior to starting the engine. Or to double check to see whether you brought the food and beverages on board. You can also remind yourself of such mundane things as bringing a bag of ice for the ice chest. You can update this list whenever you think of it.

Chores is another part of your boat book that can be developed readily and is especially useful if you have a crew or guests who want to participate. Here you can describe the routine, on-board jobs you want to have done and assign these duties. These chores can include pre-cruise belowdecks checks as to be certain all gear is secure, that there is no water in the bilge, and that the portlights are closed. Or you can itemize housekeeping chores after a cruise, such as: *Crew Member 1: Sweep cabin sole, wash dishes and put them away; Crew Member 2: Make up bunks.* And so on. That way, when you come back from an extended cruise, you have organized the chores and your vessel can get back into Bristol shape sooner with less fuss.

C**rew Members:** Here you can write down the names, addresses, and telephone numbers (home, work, or other) of your crew members so that you can reach them when you might need them—especially when the weather beckons for an impromptu cruise. But if your boat is small and doesn't carry a regular crew, you can use this section to write down the names, addresses, and telephone numbers of people you've promised yourself you'd invite on board some day. These guests then become your "crew" and you'll have a ready source of names when you're at the marina, the wind is up and the gods of the sky smile down on you.

If you have a larger boat, you can develop a **Crew Function** list. Here you can keep a central source of information on what each crew member is to do as you prepare to get underway, cruise, keep watch, or return to dock. This is a good place to list such things as: *Crew Member 1: Take sail covers off and stow below. Crew Member 2: Untie and check jib furling gear and stand by to hoist main.* And so on. You can also include your own **"heavy weather"** instructions, such as to reduce sail, secure belowdecks, don weather gear, harnesses, storm boots, and check that all hatches and ports are secure.

G**uest embarking instructions** is a good place for information you want your new on-board guests to have—especially those who have never been on a boat before. This will be information they'll want and need to enjoy their cruise if they've not had much boating experience. Here you can give them safety instructions, such as to stay off the bow when the boat is underway; to not wear spiked heels on your teak deck (maybe you keep a pair of all-size slip on footwear handy), and list various procedures on board, including instructions on how to use the head (and for that matter, what the head is and where it is located.) This is a list you probably can add a little to every time you take a new guest on board. Some skippers thoughtfully make a **machine copy** of this section and **mail it to guests** before they come on board so they'll be prepared for their time afloat, including what to bring, such as sun glasses, sun screen, a hat, deck shoes, comfortable clothing and some sort of foul-weather gear. At the end of the section is **basic nautical terms** so newcomers will better understand your boat and the nautical world they'll be entering.

Part 4 / BOATING JOURNAL

K**eeping a journal** of your boating experiences can be *useful* and *enjoyable.* By taking just a few minutes to record a little information, you can create a *special boating record* for you and your crew to use and enjoy season after season.

Your **BOAT BOOK** contains 50 *structured* **boating journals**. Each has space for you to create a *written record* of your special days afloat. You'll find that *just a few words* or facts will help you keep a pleasure record that, in combination with the navigational information you keep on your nautical chart or official log, will make your jaunt safer and be a good reference. It will also help you create a record of the boating activity and events that made your time on the water so memorable.

Each journal page is structured for your ready use. Using the *section headings* as a guide, you'll find it easy to record a word or two of pertinent information, such as your sea state, the weather, your departure time, destination, speed as well as your observations and commentaries. This journal is not a *formal ship's log*, of course, and is not intended to record hour-by-hour ship's course, hourly speed, coordinates, or a running record of sail changes or weather. But you'll find it handy to **record basic details** of your *pleasure* boating activities. You can use as many pages as you like for each cruise. And you'll find that even a few words about your boating fun, whether a few hours or a week-long cruise, will provide you with useful information and will let you recall splendid memories that will last long after the boating season.

Future cruises is your cruising *"wish list."* It's where you can write down details of interesting cruises that you might want to take someday. As you hear these ideas from boating friends or read about interesting boating adventures, jot down a few details as well as references. In a while, you'll have a list of cruises you may someday want to take. It's a good idea, too, to list any cruising recommendations you hear, such as special instructions on entering a particular harbor, things to look out for on your way in, good anchorages, or even the locations of good restaurants.

Section 5 / GETTING SHIPSHAPE

This section is designed to allow a boat owner to collect useful data to keep the vessel in top shape as well as be a source of pride. Correctly used, this book will help skippers get better work done in less time.

Spring Commissioning checklist: In this section, we present *quick reference checklists* and *action schedules*, so that a boater can quickly, but completely, go over the vessel, get organized, schedule what needs to be done, and complete the work in a minimum of time and effort.

Hull: Here the skipper can use a simple checklist to systematically go over all portions of the hull, from underwater to belowdecks. *BELOW THE WATERLINE :* checks include inspecting the rudder, condition of anodes, osmotic blistering and the condition of the bottom paint. TOPSIDES: Includes checking the ground tackle, deck fittings, winches, dock lines, cockpit drains, rigging, turnbuckles, mast and spreaders.

Belowdecks: Inspections include checking clamps and hoses, pumps, seacocks, tanks, head, hoses, seals. ENGINE: Includes checking over the engine for leaks, exhaust system rust, loose nuts, frayed belts, and hoses for softness, bulging or leaking.

Electrical: Checking the condition of batteries, inspecting wiring for loose connections, corrosion, or chafe; checking that systems work. SAFETY: includes locating and inspecting safety items such as distress flares, fire extinguisher, PFDs, whistles, and flashlights.

Fall layup: itemizes *inspection steps* to lay up the boat for winter. Like the spring commissioning section, this checklist covers all aspects of inspection for the boat owner to be aware of. This ranges from cleaning the hull, looking for specific repair items, to fall-layup procedures including winterizing the engine. Following the quick checklist is the boat owner's **Action Schedule**, in which the owner itemizes those maintenance and repair jobs he or she wants to perform at this time.

Section 6 / EMERGENCY

Here you can create your own step-by-step methods and procedures to deal with on-board **boating emergencies.** Each section begins with general *explanatory material.* From this and from your own experience and resources, you can develop your own **emergency plan.** This section contains **man overboard** information, how to make **emergency VHF** calls, what to do in case of **on-board fire**, and, lastly, emergency instructions to cope with a hull that suddenly begins **taking on water.** In each section is a diagram of the boat. Here the skipper should indicate where gear or emergency equipment is located.

Section 7 / RECORDS & SUPPLIES

Here you can keep better control of various items and stores on your boat. For example, **galley basics** is your on-board list for those things you keep routinely in the galley. There's a handy checklist for your use to tell you when to replenish supplies so you won't get caught short again. Also, there's a *shopping list* for you to work with, so that when you're onshore and purchasing supplies, you have your shopping list ready to go. You'll want a record for your **boat supplies** as well. Your **chart locker** keeps track of the on-board charts you have as well as their publication dates. There's a purchasing list here as well for you to write down information on new charts you want to order. **Rope locker** records the various types, lengths, condition and date purchased of the lines you have on board (handy to tell when a line is getting old—and should be rotated or replaced). There's also, in this section, a handy **Boat Gear Locator.** This lets you record the place where you *store various important pieces* of boat gear. For example, if you use this section, you can safely put away that bilge pump repair kit under the cabin sole, you'll be able to locate it quickly when you need it. **Names and addresses** is that handy place where you can keep track of some of the friendly people you meet in marinas, in anchorages, or various places with your boat. Just jot down their names, addresses, and how to keep in contact with them in this section.

Expenditures is a place to record your *boat's costs*, including the cost of new equipment, replacement gear, insurance, docking charges, slip costs, insurance fees, repairs, and fuel. With this information, you can set up a proper budget. If you use your vessel for business, this can be an invaluable record, along with other records, for your financial records.

Your boating **Appointments and schedules** lets you keep better information on dates and times specifically relating to your boat, such as your appointment for your next haul out, or when your slip rental fee comes due. Or jot down when you have scheduled your next guests to come on board. You can use it in many ways as a handy organizer of boating dates and times.

In all, your BOAT BOOK can be an important source of *organization, information, help* and *inspiration* to your boating work and pleasure. Use it carefully, for it will reward you in *better boating and safety.* And it'll help you get you more and better time on the water.

Section 2

BOAT ORGANIZER

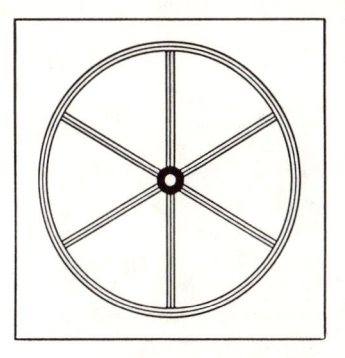

Boat specifications & data

Boat equipment record

Major suppliers

To do projects

Purchasing organizer & record

My workbook

Boat basic specifications

Name of boat   Date commissioned

Registration   Owner

Boat Manufacturer

Address

City   State   Zip

Telephone number

Purchased from: Date

Address

City   State   Zip

Telephone Numbers

☆ Specifications

Length overall   Length on the water line

Beam   Draft

Freeboard   Mast height above water

Weight   Hull material   Colors

Manufacturer's hull number   Sail identification

Number passengers   Water tank capacity:

☆ Power

Engine Builder

Address

City   State   Zip

Telephone Number

Engine serial number

Fuel type: Fuel capacity:

Spark plug   Fan belt   Filters

Other:

Top or theoretical hull speed   Best day's run

☆ Sailboat only:

Ballast weight   Sail Area: Main   Jib   Other

Main L=   P=   **Jib** L=   P=   **Other** L=:   P=

Key Sailboat Performance Ratios*:

SA/D Sail area to displacement ratio:
D/WL Displacement to waterline ratio:
B/D Ballast to displacement ratio:
Hull theoretical speed:

☆ ☆

*Design ratios:
 Sail area/ displacement—under 14, low; 14 to 17, moderate; 18-21 high; above 21, very high
Ballast to displacement ratio, under 30%, low; 30 to 40%, moderate; 40 to 50%, high; over 50%, very high
Displacement to waterline, below 100, ultralight; 100 to 200, lightweight; 200-300, generally considerate a mediumweight; over 300, heavyweight vessel.

Boat Equipment Record

Major equipment items, descriptions and serial numbers

Here is where you maintain your record of major equipment aboard as well as a description and serial number. Keep a separate machine copy in a safe place. If an item is missing, stolen, lost or damaged, these are records to identify your boating item or use as a basis for an insurance claim.

Equipment item	Description	Serial Number
1/		
2/		
3/		
4/		
5/		
6/		
7/		
8/		
9/		
10/		
11/		
12/		
13/		
14/		

15/

16/

17/

18/

19/

20/

21/

22/

23/

24/

25/

26/

27/

28/

29/

30/

31/

32/

33/

34/

35/

Major suppliers

Your record of major suppliers: names, addresses and telephone numbers

Here you keep the information you need to get parts, service, or information from the people you routinely buy from: ship's stores, catalog houses, manufacturers and suppliers, specialists, or sail makers. It's useful to keep this list up to date so you have one centralized source for information.

Name

Address

City   State   Zip

Telephone

Purchases

Name

Address

City   State   Zip

Telephone

Purchases

Name

Address

City   State   Zip

Telephone

Purchases

Name

Address

City   State   Zip

Telephone

Purchases

Name

Address

City   State   Zip

Telephone

Purchases

★ ★ ★ ★ ★ ★

To do list

This is your list of what you want to do on your boat. Here you can write down items to repair, upgrade or maintain your vessel. (Note: If your projects involve new purchases, be certain to also list those things you want to buy in your **Purchasing organizer and record**). For example, your to do list might be: "revarnish cabin sole." Your purchase list then would be: "order quart of varnish."

1/

2/

3/

4/

5/

6/

7/

8/

9/

10/

11/

12/

13/

14/

15/

16/
17/
18/
19/
20/
21/
22/
23/
24/
25/
26/
27/
28/
29/
30/
31/
32/
33/
34/
35/

Purchasing organizer & record

Items you want to purchase for your boat, along with pertinent specifications. This is your boat's "shopping list" for you to buy while you are on shore.

Item	Description	Price
1/		
2/		
3/		
4/		
5/		
6/		
7/		
8/		
9/		
10/		
11/		
12/		
13/		
14/		
15/		
16/		

17/
18/
19/
20/
21/
22/
23/
24/
25/
26/
27/
28/
29/
30/
31/
32/
33/
34/
35/
36/
37/

My Workbook

Here you can describe and sketch some of the **ideas** you want to develop for your boat. Use these pages to begin your thinking. For example, you might want a new shelf in the cabin. You would begin by writing in the top of the space, *"New Cabin Shelf."* Take measurements of the area where the shelf will be located; then draw the shelf below. As you work with your ideas, add in the details of what you'll need: 1/ dimensions 2/ wood to be purchased 3/ screws 4/ glue 5/ oil finish Then complete your Boat Book **To do** list (write: add cabin shelf) and in your **Boat Book Purchasing organizer**, write the materials and supplies you need.

Idea 1

Idea 2

Idea 3

Idea 4

Idea 5

Idea 6

Idea 7

Idea 8

Section 3:

Cruise Organizer

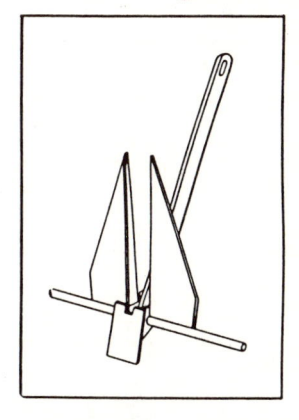

Getting ready to go

Chores: before & after

Crew members

Crew functions

Watch duty

Guest embarking instructions

Getting ready to go

Your checklist of items to remember as you prepare to shove off

1/
2/
3/
4/
5/
6/
7/
8/
9/
10/
11/
12/
13/
14/
15/
16/
17/
18/

19/
20/
21/
22/
23/
24/
25/
26/
27/
28/
29/
30/
31/
32/
33/
34/
35/
36/
37/
38/
40/

Chores

Here is the place to list various chores and procedures that need to be done before, during, or after a cruise. You can organize these and assign them to various crew members or guests.

	Crew 1	Crew 2	Crew 3	Crew 4
Chore:				
1/				
2/				
3/				
4/				
5/				
6/				
7/				
8/				
9/				
10/				
11/				
12/				
13/				
14/				
15/				

16/ ....

17/ ....

18/ ....

19/ ....

20/ ....

21/ ....

22/ ....

23/ ....

24/ ....

25/ ....

26/ ....

27/ ....

28/ ....

29/ ....

30/ ....

31/ ....

32/ ....

33/ ....

34/ ....

35/ ....

36/ ....

Crew Members

Your record of crew members names, addresses and home and office telephone numbers (and alternate telephone numbers)

Name

Address

City   State   Zip

Home telephone   Office   Other:

Special information

Name

Address

City   State   Zip

Home telephone   Office: Other:

Special information

Name

Address

City   State   Zip

Home telephone   Office: Other:

Special information

Name

Address

City　　　　　　　　　State　　　　　Zip

Home telephone　　　　Office:　　　　Other:

Special information

Name

Address

City　　　　　　　　　State　　　　　Zip

Home telephone　　　　Office:　　　　Other:

Special information

Name

Address

City　　　　　　　　　State　　　　　Zip

Home telephone　　　　Office:　　　　Other:

Special information

★ ★

Name

Address

City　　　　　　　　　　State　　　　Zip

Home telephone　　　　　Office:　　　Other:

Special information

Name

Address

City　　　　　　　　　　State　　　　Zip

Home telephone　　　　　Office:　　　Other:

Special information

Name

Address

City　　　　　　　　　　State　　　　Zip

Home telephone　　　　　Office:　　　Other:

Special information

★ ★ ★ Crew duties list ★ ★ ★

Crew names and assignments:

DUTY	CREW MEMBER
1/	
2/	
3/	
4/	
5/	
6/	
7/	
8/	

Shoving off

9/	
10/	
11/	
12/	
13/	

Cruising

14/	
15	
16/	

17/

18/

Heavy weather

19/

20/

21/

22/

23/

24/

26/

27/

28/

29/

30/

Return to shore

31/

32/

33/

34/

35/

36/

37

☆ ☆ ☆ ☆ ☆

Watch Schedules

Crew members and watch duties

Assign **Crew Members** and determine the **watch hour frequency** (every 4 hours or 6 hours, for example). Then write in the exact **time** of each watch (in 24-hour system): Example: **Watch 1**: 0000 (midnight) to 0600 (6 a.m.); **Watch 2**: 0601 to 1200 (noon). Under **Day**, combine **Watch number** with **crew number**. For example, Crew Member 1 (Bill) has Watch 1, which means he will be on duty on Day 1 from midnight to 6 a.m.) You can rotate this schedule through a series of cruising days so everyone has a "good" watch. (**Note:** you can make advance machine copies to hand out).

Names: Crew Member #1_____ #2_____
#3_____ #4_____ #5_____

Watch Hour Frequency: Every _____ hours

Times: Watch 1/ From _____ To_____ **Watch 2/** From_____ To_____
Watch 3/ From _____ To_____ **Watch 4/** From_____ To_____ **Watch 5/** From _____ To_____ **Watch 6/** From_____ To_____ **Additional**_____

Daily Schedule

Day #_____ Watch 1_____ Watch 2_____ Watch 3_____
Watch 4_____ Watch 5_____ Watch 6_____

Day #_____ Watch 1_____ Watch 2_____ Watch 3_____
Watch 4_____ Watch 5_____ Watch 6_____

Day #_____ Watch 1_____ Watch 2_____ Watch 3_____
Watch 4_____ Watch 5_____ Watch 6_____

Day #_____ Watch 1_____ Watch 2_____ Watch 3_____
Watch 4_____ Watch 5_____ Watch 6_____

Day #_____ Watch 1_____ Watch 2_____ Watch 3_____
Watch 4_____ Watch 5_____ Watch 6_____

Repeat Watches as follows :

Welcome Aboard!

Guest embarking suggestions and helpful information

Boat Name: **Type:**
Time & date aboard   Boat slip number
How to find our boat

Welcome! We look forward to seeing you and we hope to have a great time with you on the water. For you to have a pleasant experience aboard, we are sending the following basic boating information and suggestions on appropriate equipment. *Please feel free to ask questions.*

Please bring the following gear for your comfort:

For your information while on board:

BASIC BOAT TERMS: Forward (toward the front of the boat)/ **Aft** (rear of the boat)/ **Head** (toilet area)/ **Helm** (steering device)/ **Berth** (the bed aboard a boat)/ **Boom** (horizontal part of the mast on a sailboat) / **Mast** (the big pole sticking up from the deck of a sailboat that holds the sails)/ **Cast off** (to release the boat from the dock by untying the lines)/ **Cleat** (where lines are tied)/ **Lines** (what boaters call ropes) **Douse the sails** (lower the sails)/ **Foredeck** (forward part of the deck, near the bow)/ **Cockpit** (the area where people sit)/ **Knot** (nautical speed equal to 1.15 miles per hour)./ **Galley** (kitchen area)/ **Halyard** (line used to raise a sail)/ **Hatch** (cover over an opening in the deck)/ **Heel** (the boat's lean when wind blows hard)/ **Mainsail** (the big sail)/ **Jib** (the smaller sail ahead of the mainsail)/ **Port** (the left side of the boat)/ **Starboard** (the right side)/ **Windward** (the direction the wind is blowing from)/ **Leeward** (the direction the wind is blowing toward)/ **Berthing** (the cruise is over)

Signed: _____Captain

Section 4

BOATING JOURNAL

50-cruise structured journal

Dates / times / weather / sea state

cruising log / observations / expenses

Future cruises

CRUISE NUMBER _____   BOAT BOOK

BOATING JOURNAL

DATE   Destination
Weather: Temperature:
Wind: Visibility: Sea Conditions:

Entry:

....
....
....
....
....
....
....
....
....
....

Time cruise completed: Days's run (miles):   Average speed:
Fuel on board: Engine hours or total time:
Unusual events / observations:

Guests on board:
For tax records if applicable: Business conducted onboard

Expense record: $

Skipper

BOAT BOOK   CRUISE NUMBER _____

BOATING JOURNAL

DATE
Weather:
Wind:
Destination
Temperature:
Visibility:
Sea Conditions:

Entry:

....

....

....

....

....

....

....

....

....

....

Time cruise completed: Days's run (miles):   Average speed:
Fuel on board: Engine hours or total time:
Unusual events / observations:

Guests on board:
For tax records if applicable: Business conducted onboard

Expense record: $

Skipper

CRUISE NUMBER _____   BOAT BOOK

BOATING JOURNAL

DATE   Destination
Weather: Temperature:
Wind: Visibility: Sea Conditions:

Entry:

....
....
....
....
....
....
....
....
....
....

Time cruise completed: Days's run (miles):   Average speed:
Fuel on board: Engine hours or total time:
Unusual events / observations:

Guests on board:
For tax records if applicable: Business conducted onboard

Expense record: $

Skipper

BOAT BOOK   CRUISE NUMBER _____

BOATING JOURNAL

DATE   Destination
Weather: Temperature:
Wind: Visibility: Sea Conditions:

Entry:

....

....

....

....

....

....

....

....

....

....

Time cruise completed: Days's run (miles):   Average speed:
Fuel on board: Engine hours or total time:
Unusual events / observations:

Guests on board:
For tax records if applicable: Business conducted onboard

Expense record: $

Skipper

CRUISE NUMBER _____   BOAT BOOK

BOATING JOURNAL

DATE
Weather:
Wind:
Destination
Temperature:
Visibility:
Sea Conditions:

Entry:

....
....
....
....
....
....
....
....
....
....
....

Time cruise completed: Days's run (miles):   Average speed:
Fuel on board: Engine hours or total time:
Unusual events / observations:

Guests on board:
For tax records if applicable: Business conducted onboard

Expense record: $

Skipper

BOAT BOOK   CRUISE NUMBER _____

BOATING JOURNAL

DATE   Destination
Weather: Temperature:
Wind: Visibility: Sea Conditions:

Entry:

....

....

....

....

....

....

....

....

....

....

Time cruise completed: Days's run (miles):   Average speed:
Fuel on board: Engine hours or total time:
Unusual events / observations:

Guests on board:
For tax records if applicable: Business conducted onboard

Expense record: $

Skipper

CRUISE NUMBER _____   BOAT BOOK

BOATING JOURNAL

DATE   Destination
Weather: Temperature:
Wind: Visibility: Sea Conditions:

Entry:

....
....
....
....
....
....
....
....
....
....

Time cruise completed: Days's run (miles):   Average speed:
Fuel on board: Engine hours or total time:
Unusual events / observations:

Guests on board:
For tax records if applicable: Business conducted onboard

Expense record: $

Skipper

BOAT BOOK   CRUISE NUMBER _____

BOATING JOURNAL

DATE
Weather:
Wind:

Destination
Temperature:
Visibility:

Sea Conditions:

Entry:

....
....
....
....
....
....
....
....
....
....

Time cruise completed: Days's run (miles):   Average speed:
Fuel on board: Engine hours or total time:
Unusual events / observations:

Guests on board:
For tax records if applicable: Business conducted onboard

Expense record: $

Skipper

CRUISE NUMBER _____ BOAT BOOK

BOATING JOURNAL

DATE
Weather:
Wind:
Destination
Temperature:
Visibility:
Sea Conditions:

Entry:

....

....

....

....

....

....

....

....

....

....

Time cruise completed: Days's run (miles):   Average speed:
Fuel on board: Engine hours or total time:
Unusual events / observations:

Guests on board:
For tax records if applicable: Business conducted onboard

Expense record: $

Skipper

BOAT BOOK   CRUISE NUMBER _____

BOATING JOURNAL

DATE
Weather:
Wind:

Destination
Temperature:
Visibility:

Sea Conditions:

Entry:

....
....
....
....
....
....
....
....
....
....
....

Time cruise completed: Days's run (miles):   Average speed:
Fuel on board: Engine hours or total time:
Unusual events / observations:

Guests on board:
For tax records if applicable: Business conducted onboard

Expense record: $

Skipper

CRUISE NUMBER _____   BOAT BOOK

BOATING JOURNAL

DATE   Destination
Weather: Temperature:
Wind: Visibility: Sea Conditions:

Entry:

....
....
....
....
....
....
....
....
....
....

Time cruise completed: Days's run (miles):   Average speed:
Fuel on board: Engine hours or total time:
Unusual events / observations:

Guests on board:
For tax records if applicable: Business conducted onboard

Expense record: $

Skipper

BOAT BOOK   CRUISE NUMBER _____

BOATING JOURNAL

DATE   Destination
Weather: Temperature:
Wind: Visibility: Sea Conditions:

Entry:

....

....

....

....

....

....

....

....

....

....

....

Time cruise completed: Days's run (miles):   Average speed:
Fuel on board: Engine hours or total time:
Unusual events / observations:

Guests on board:
For tax records if applicable: Business conducted onboard

Expense record: $

Skipper

CRUISE NUMBER _____ BOAT BOOK

BOATING JOURNAL

DATE
Weather:
Wind:

Destination
Temperature:
Visibility: Sea Conditions:

Entry:

....

....

....

....

....

....

....

....

....

....

Time cruise completed: Days's run (miles):   Average speed:
Fuel on board: Engine hours or total time:
Unusual events / observations:

Guests on board:
For tax records if applicable: Business conducted onboard

Expense record: $

Skipper

BOAT BOOK   CRUISE NUMBER _____

BOATING JOURNAL

DATE   Destination
Weather: Temperature:
Wind: Visibility: Sea Conditions:

Entry:

....

....

....

....

....

....

....

....

....

....

Time cruise completed: Days's run (miles):   Average speed:
Fuel on board: Engine hours or total time:
Unusual events / observations:

Guests on board:
For tax records if applicable: Business conducted onboard

Expense record: $

Skipper

CRUISE NUMBER _____   BOAT BOOK

BOATING JOURNAL

DATE
Weather:
Wind:

Destination
Temperature:
Visibility: Sea Conditions:

Entry:

....
....
....
....
....
....
....
....
....
....

Time cruise completed: Days's run (miles):   Average speed:
Fuel on board: Engine hours or total time:
Unusual events / observations:

Guests on board:
For tax records if applicable: Business conducted onboard

Expense record: $

Skipper

BOAT BOOK   CRUISE NUMBER _____

BOATING JOURNAL

DATE
Weather:
Wind:

Destination
Temperature:
Visibility:

Sea Conditions:

Entry:

....

....

....

....

....

....

....

....

....

....

Time cruise completed: Days's run (miles):   Average speed:
Fuel on board: Engine hours or total time:
Unusual events / observations:

Guests on board:
For tax records if applicable: Business conducted onboard

Expense record: $

Skipper

CRUISE NUMBER _____   BOAT BOOK

BOATING JOURNAL

DATE
Weather:
Wind:

Destination
Temperature:
Visibility: Sea Conditions:

Entry:

....
....
....
....
....
....
....
....
....
....

Time cruise completed: Days's run (miles):   Average speed:
Fuel on board: Engine hours or total time:
Unusual events / observations:

Guests on board:
For tax records if applicable: Business conducted onboard

Expense record: $

Skipper

BOAT BOOK   CRUISE NUMBER _____

BOATING JOURNAL

DATE   Destination
Weather: Temperature:
Wind: Visibility: Sea Conditions:

Entry:

....

....

....

....

....

....

....

....

....

....

Time cruise completed: Days's run (miles):   Average speed:
Fuel on board: Engine hours or total time:
Unusual events / observations:

Guests on board:
For tax records if applicable: Business conducted onboard

Expense record: $

Skipper

CRUISE NUMBER _____   BOAT BOOK

BOATING JOURNAL

DATE   Destination
Weather: Temperature:
Wind: Visibility: Sea Conditions:

Entry:

....

....

....

....

....

....

....

....

....

....

....

Time cruise completed: Days's run (miles):   Average speed:
Fuel on board: Engine hours or total time:
Unusual events / observations:

Guests on board:
For tax records if applicable: Business conducted onboard

Expense record: $

Skipper

BOAT BOOK   CRUISE NUMBER _____

BOATING JOURNAL

DATE
Weather:
Wind:

Destination
Temperature:
Visibility:

Sea Conditions:

Entry:

....

....

....

....

....

....

....

....

....

....

Time cruise completed: Days's run (miles):   Average speed:
Fuel on board: Engine hours or total time:
Unusual events / observations:

Guests on board:
For tax records if applicable: Business conducted onboard

Expense record: $

Skipper

CRUISE NUMBER _____   BOAT BOOK

BOATING JOURNAL

DATE
Weather:
Wind:

Destination
Temperature:
Visibility: Sea Conditions:

Entry:

....

....

....

....

....

....

....

....

....

....

Time cruise completed: Days's run (miles):   Average speed:
Fuel on board: Engine hours or total time:
Unusual events / observations:

Guests on board:
For tax records if applicable: Business conducted onboard

Expense record: $

Skipper

BOAT BOOK   CRUISE NUMBER _____

BOATING JOURNAL

DATE
Weather:
Wind:

Destination
Temperature:
Visibility:

Sea Conditions:

Entry:

....
....
....
....
....
....
....
....
....
....
....

Time cruise completed: Days's run (miles):   Average speed:
Fuel on board: Engine hours or total time:
Unusual events / observations:

Guests on board:
For tax records if applicable: Business conducted onboard

Expense record: $

Skipper

CRUISE NUMBER _____   BOAT BOOK

BOATING JOURNAL

DATE
Weather:
Wind:

Destination
Temperature:
Visibility: Sea Conditions:

Entry:

Time cruise completed: Days's run (miles):   Average speed:
Fuel on board: Engine hours or total time:
Unusual events / observations:

Guests on board:
For tax records if applicable: Business conducted onboard

Expense record: $

Skipper

BOAT BOOK   CRUISE NUMBER _____

BOATING JOURNAL

DATE   Destination
Weather: Temperature:
Wind: Visibility: Sea Conditions:

Entry:

....
....
....
....
....
....
....
....
....
....
....
....

Time cruise completed: Days's run (miles):   Average speed:
Fuel on board: Engine hours or total time:
Unusual events / observations:

Guests on board:
For tax records if applicable: Business conducted onboard

Expense record: $

Skipper

CRUISE NUMBER _____   BOAT BOOK

BOATING JOURNAL

DATE
Weather:
Wind:

Destination
Temperature:
Visibility: Sea Conditions:

Entry:

....

....

....

....

....

....

....

....

....

....

Time cruise completed: Days's run (miles):   Average speed:
Fuel on board: Engine hours or total time:
Unusual events / observations:

Guests on board:
For tax records if applicable: Business conducted onboard

Expense record: $

Skipper

BOAT BOOK   CRUISE NUMBER _____

BOATING JOURNAL

DATE   Destination
Weather: Temperature:
Wind: Visibility: Sea Conditions:

Entry:

....

....

....

....

....

....

....

....

....

....

....

Time cruise completed: Days's run (miles):   Average speed:
Fuel on board: Engine hours or total time:
Unusual events / observations:

Guests on board:
For tax records if applicable: Business conducted onboard

Expense record: $

Skipper

CRUISE NUMBER _____   BOAT BOOK

BOATING JOURNAL

DATE
Weather:
Wind:

Destination
Temperature:
Visibility:

Sea Conditions:

Entry:

....
....
....
....
....
....
....
....
....
....
....

Time cruise completed: Days's run (miles):   Average speed:
Fuel on board: Engine hours or total time:
Unusual events / observations:

Guests on board:
For tax records if applicable: Business conducted onboard

Expense record: $

Skipper

BOAT BOOK CRUISE NUMBER _____

BOATING JOURNAL

DATE Destination
Weather: Temperature:
Wind: Visibility: Sea Conditions:

Entry:

....

....

....

....

....

....

....

....

....

....

Time cruise completed: Days's run (miles): Average speed:
Fuel on board: Engine hours or total time:
Unusual events / observations:

Guests on board:
For tax records if applicable: Business conducted onboard

Expense record: $

Skipper

CRUISE NUMBER _____   BOAT BOOK

BOATING JOURNAL

DATE   Destination
Weather: Temperature:
Wind: Visibility: Sea Conditions:

Entry:

Time cruise completed: Days's run (miles):   Average speed:
Fuel on board: Engine hours or total time:
Unusual events / observations:

Guests on board:
For tax records if applicable: Business conducted onboard

Expense record: $

Skipper

BOAT BOOK   CRUISE NUMBER _____

BOATING JOURNAL

DATE
Weather:
Wind:

Destination
Temperature:
Visibility:

Sea Conditions:

Entry:

....

....

....

....

....

....

....

....

....

....

....

Time cruise completed: Days's run (miles):   Average speed:
Fuel on board: Engine hours or total time:
Unusual events / observations:

Guests on board:
For tax records if applicable: Business conducted onboard

Expense record: $

Skipper

CRUISE NUMBER _____   BOAT BOOK

BOATING JOURNAL

DATE   Destination
Weather: Temperature:
Wind: Visibility: Sea Conditions:

Entry:

....

....

....

....

....

....

....

....

....

....

Time cruise completed: Days's run (miles):   Average speed:
Fuel on board: Engine hours or total time:
Unusual events / observations:

Guests on board:
For tax records if applicable: Business conducted onboard

Expense record: $

Skipper

BOAT BOOK   CRUISE NUMBER _____

BOATING JOURNAL

DATE
Weather:
Wind:

Destination
Temperature:
Visibility:

Sea Conditions:

Entry:

....

....

....

....

....

....

....

....

....

....

Time cruise completed: Days's run (miles):   Average speed:
Fuel on board: Engine hours or total time:
Unusual events / observations:

Guests on board:
For tax records if applicable: Business conducted onboard

Expense record: $

Skipper

CRUISE NUMBER _____   BOAT BOOK

BOATING JOURNAL

DATE   Destination
Weather: Temperature:
Wind: Visibility: Sea Conditions:

Entry:

....

....

....

....

....

....

....

....

....

....

Time cruise completed: Days's run (miles):   Average speed:
Fuel on board: Engine hours or total time:
Unusual events / observations:

Guests on board:
For tax records if applicable: Business conducted onboard

Expense record: $

Skipper

BOAT BOOK   CRUISE NUMBER _____

BOATING JOURNAL

DATE
Weather:
Wind:

Destination
Temperature:
Visibility:

Sea Conditions:

Entry:

....

....

....

....

....

....

....

....

....

....

Time cruise completed: Days's run (miles):   Average speed:
Fuel on board: Engine hours or total time:
Unusual events / observations:

Guests on board:
For tax records if applicable: Business conducted onboard

Expense record: $

Skipper

CRUISE NUMBER _____   BOAT BOOK

BOATING JOURNAL

DATE
Weather:
Wind:

Destination
Temperature:
Visibility: Sea Conditions:

Entry:

....

....

....

....

....

....

....

....

....

....

Time cruise completed: Days's run (miles):   Average speed:
Fuel on board: Engine hours or total time:
Unusual events / observations:

Guests on board:
For tax records if applicable: Business conducted onboard

Expense record: $

Skipper

BOAT BOOK   CRUISE NUMBER _____

BOATING JOURNAL

DATE
Weather:
Wind:

Destination
Temperature:
Visibility:

Sea Conditions:

Entry:

....

....

....

....

....

....

....

....

....

....

Time cruise completed: Days's run (miles):   Average speed:
Fuel on board: Engine hours or total time:
Unusual events / observations:

Guests on board:
For tax records if applicable: Business conducted onboard

Expense record: $

Skipper

CRUISE NUMBER _____   BOAT BOOK

BOATING JOURNAL

DATE   Destination
Weather: Temperature:
Wind: Visibility: Sea Conditions:

Entry:

....
....
....
....
....
....
....
....
....
....

Time cruise completed: Days's run (miles):   Average speed:
Fuel on board: Engine hours or total time:
Unusual events / observations:

Guests on board:
For tax records if applicable: Business conducted onboard

Expense record: $

Skipper

BOAT BOOK CRUISE NUMBER _____

BOATING JOURNAL

DATE
Weather:
Wind:

Destination
Temperature:
Visibility:

Sea Conditions:

Entry:

....

....

....

....

....

....

....

....

....

Time cruise completed: Days's run (miles):   Average speed:
Fuel on board: Engine hours or total time:
Unusual events / observations:

Guests on board:
For tax records if applicable: Business conducted onboard

Expense record: $

Skipper

CRUISE NUMBER _____   BOAT BOOK

BOATING JOURNAL

DATE   Destination
Weather: Temperature:
Wind: Visibility: Sea Conditions:

Entry:

....

....

....

....

....

....

....

....

....

Time cruise completed: Days's run (miles):   Average speed:
Fuel on board: Engine hours or total time:
Unusual events / observations:

Guests on board:
For tax records if applicable: Business conducted onboard

Expense record: $

Skipper

BOAT BOOK   CRUISE NUMBER _____

BOATING JOURNAL

DATE   Destination
Weather: Temperature:
Wind: Visibility: Sea Conditions:

Entry:

....
....
....
....
....
....
....
....
....
....

Time cruise completed: Days's run (miles):   Average speed:
Fuel on board: Engine hours or total time:
Unusual events / observations:

Guests on board:
For tax records if applicable: Business conducted onboard

Expense record: $

Skipper

CRUISE NUMBER _____   BOAT BOOK

BOATING JOURNAL

DATE   Destination
Weather: Temperature:
Wind: Visibility: Sea Conditions:

Entry:

....

....

....

....

....

....

....

....

....

....

Time cruise completed: Days's run (miles):   Average speed:
Fuel on board: Engine hours or total time:
Unusual events / observations:

Guests on board:
For tax records if applicable: Business conducted onboard

Expense record: $

Skipper

BOAT BOOK   CRUISE NUMBER _____

BOATING JOURNAL

DATE
Weather:
Wind:

Destination
Temperature:
Visibility:

Sea Conditions:

Entry:

....
....
....
....
....
....
....
....
....
....

Time cruise completed: Days's run (miles):   Average speed:
Fuel on board: Engine hours or total time:
Unusual events / observations:

Guests on board:
For tax records if applicable: Business conducted onboard

Expense record: $

Skipper

CRUISE NUMBER _____   BOAT BOOK

BOATING JOURNAL

DATE
Weather:
Wind:

Destination
Temperature:
Visibility: Sea Conditions:

Entry:

....
....
....
....
....
....
....
....
....
....

Time cruise completed: Days's run (miles):   Average speed:
Fuel on board: Engine hours or total time:
Unusual events / observations:

Guests on board:
For tax records if applicable: Business conducted onboard

Expense record: $

Skipper

BOAT BOOK   CRUISE NUMBER _____

BOATING JOURNAL

DATE
Weather:
Wind:

Destination
Temperature:
Visibility:

Sea Conditions:

Entry:

....

....

....

....

....

....

....

....

....

....

Time cruise completed: Days's run (miles):   Average speed:
Fuel on board: Engine hours or total time:
Unusual events / observations:

Guests on board:
For tax records if applicable: Business conducted onboard

Expense record: $

Skipper

CRUISE NUMBER _____ BOAT BOOK

BOATING JOURNAL

DATE
Weather:
Wind:

Destination
Temperature:
Visibility:

Sea Conditions:

Entry:

....

....

....

....

....

....

....

....

....

....

Time cruise completed: Days's run (miles):   Average speed:
Fuel on board: Engine hours or total time:
Unusual events / observations:

Guests on board:
For tax records if applicable: Business conducted onboard

Expense record: $

Skipper

BOAT BOOK   CRUISE NUMBER _____

BOATING JOURNAL

DATE
Weather:
Wind:

Destination
Temperature:
Visibility:

Sea Conditions:

Entry:

....

....

....

....

....

....

....

....

....

Time cruise completed: Days's run (miles):   Average speed:
Fuel on board: Engine hours or total time:
Unusual events / observations:

Guests on board:
For tax records if applicable: Business conducted onboard

Expense record: $

Skipper

CRUISE NUMBER _____   BOAT BOOK

BOATING JOURNAL

DATE   Destination
Weather: Temperature:
Wind: Visibility: Sea Conditions:

Entry:

....

....

....

....

....

....

....

....

....

....

....

Time cruise completed: Days's run (miles):   Average speed:
Fuel on board: Engine hours or total time:
Unusual events / observations:

Guests on board:
For tax records if applicable: Business conducted onboard

Expense record: $

Skipper

BOAT BOOK   CRUISE NUMBER _____

BOATING JOURNAL

DATE   Destination
Weather: Temperature:
Wind: Visibility: Sea Conditions:

Entry:

....

....

....

....

....

....

....

....

....

....

....

Time cruise completed: Days's run (miles):   Average speed:
Fuel on board: Engine hours or total time:
Unusual events / observations:

Guests on board:
For tax records if applicable: Business conducted onboard

Expense record: $

Skipper

CRUISE NUMBER _____   BOAT BOOK

BOATING JOURNAL

DATE
Weather:
Wind:

Destination
Temperature:
Visibility: Sea Conditions:

Entry:

....

....

....

....

....

....

....

....

....

....

Time cruise completed: Days's run (miles):   Average speed:
Fuel on board: Engine hours or total time:
Unusual events / observations:

Guests on board:
For tax records if applicable: Business conducted onboard

Expense record: $

Skipper

BOAT BOOK   CRUISE NUMBER _____

BOATING JOURNAL

DATE   Destination
Weather: Temperature:
Wind: Visibility: Sea Conditions:

Entry:

....

....

....

....

....

....

....

....

....

....

Time cruise completed: Days's run (miles):   Average speed:
Fuel on board: Engine hours or total time:
Unusual events / observations:

Guests on board:
For tax records if applicable: Business conducted onboard

Expense record: $

Skipper

Future Cruises

List of cruises to take someday: Destinations, remarks & information source for future reference

Cruise # 1:

Cruise # 2:

Cruise # 3:

Cruise # 4:

Section 5

Getting Shipshape

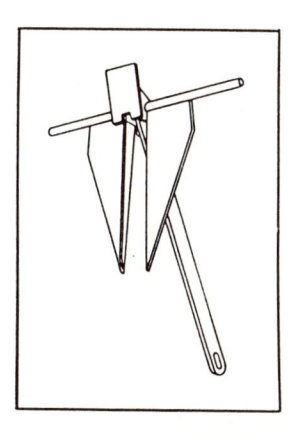

Spring commissioning checklist

Spring action schedule

Fall layup and storage checklist

Fall action schedule

★ ★ Spring commissioning ★ ★

Checklist to get ready

This is your spring organizer to inspect your boat to get it ready to put it in the water. Use the **Spring commissioning checklist** as a *general and quick guideline* to look for problems; use the Spring action schedule (page 100) to *write down specific work* that needs to be done. Also write down the *supplies and tools* you will need to order in the Purchasing organizer and record section (page 26).

General cleanup checklist:

___**Cleaning overall**—sweep down and scrub deck, cockpit/___Get carpet remnant to lay next to boat to keep boat clean/ ___Clean out drains, scuppers/ ___Check bilge/___Remove spots on deck/ cockpit/ cabin sole or elsewhere as noted / ___Fiberglass needs cleaning and polishing / ___ Refinish teak/ ___Polish stainless and chrome fittings/___Clean and polish Plexiglass/ ___Interior needs cleaning and oiling/waving/varnishing

Hull-below the waterline:

___**Check areas** which may have been subject to unusual pressures or have impact damage /___Check condition of anodes—replace sacrificial zincs/___Nicks, gouges, scrapes as noted for filling & refinishing/___Osmotic blisters—grind out and fill / ___Crazing, cracks in fiberglass as noted/___Check rudder & condition of fittings/___ Antifouling paint condition—needs replacement/ touch-up /___ Check propeller for nicks, bent blades—have serviced / ___For inboard engine, check shaft strut and cutlass bearing

Hull-topsides

___**Gelcoat** cracks or crazing—need to refinish/ ___Check for stress or other fiberglass cracks anywhere, particularly around chainplates, cleats or equipment/___ If balsa or wood core deck, check and repair small damage leading to water entry or delamination /___Double-check hull-deck join—no looseness or signs of letting go /___Double-check deck or other area oilcanning or excessive springiness /___ Need for refinishing or touch up as noted: ___oil,___ paint or___varnish /___Hatches, ports and portlights—Check for leaks around bedding compound/___General hull abrasions and worn or faded gelcoat—check and gelcoat or add new finish /___Deck leaks—check belowdecks for water marks. Trace the leak to its source and remove the fitting, repair damage, and rebed

Belowdecks

___Check seacock conditions—check for operation out of water/___Hoses—in good condition, including firmness around clamps /___Clamps—check for condition and tightness. Replace any rusted clamps /___Check tanks and fittings for overall condition/___Unusual water or oil stains—other indicators of leaks and problems /___Stuffing box—check for leaks. / ___Check keelbolts, other fasteners / ____Check chainplate through fastening. If chainplates are bolted to a bulkhead, which in turn is glassed to the hull, check the fiberglassed-in area for signs of stress, cracks, or "working."

Equipment topsides

___**Ground tackle**—in good shape /___ Deck fittings—on tightly, through bolts on securely, and no stress cracks or delamination Check bedding for water tightness /___Winches—dissemble, clean, grease & reassemble /___ Blocks--free-wheeling and clean. Oil or grease as necessary /___**Steering gear**—check for wear and smooth operation as you run it all the way side to side. *Wheel steering:*___Check cable for looseness, kinking or signs of wear, such as frayed or broken strands;___check bolts and nuts for tightness/ ___inspect pulleys and quadrants. ___Check fittings for cracks, wear, or broken teeth.___Clean, grease and oil/ ___readjust cable tension/___Check attachment to rudder. *Tiller:* ___ Check pintles and gudgeons as well as their through-bolting for solidity / ___ Check condition of tiller arm, head assembly/ ___Cockpit drains—open and free of obstruction/ ___Lines—check for wear, age, need for rotating or replacement / ___Fenders—need cleaning or replacement /___*Lifelines and stanchions*—Check the bases for solidity/ ___Check condition of sealant—are leaks coming through/___Check the fiberglass for cracks or delamination/___Check the welds for cracks/ ___Inspect the turnbuckles—replace if bent /___Check the wires for fraying or wear /___Clean, polish stanchions

Mast & rigging

___**Mast—check overall** condition—no damage or signs of fatigue or corrosion/ ___Spreaders—solid to mast, no cracks or looseness /___Spreader tips—check chafe tape, spreader boots and condition of shrouds/___Winch—check for smooth operation, need for lube/ ___Rivets or screws holding fittings are solid and have no rust or corrosion /___Cleanliness & smoothness of sail track /___Rigging and turnbuckles—check for broken strands, bent turnbuckles, other damage. Replace/ ___Inspect for hairline cracks—if warranted, check rig with chemical spray which shows cracks or faults / ___Masthead fittings and pulleys—check for looseness, corrosion, fatigue /___Cotter pins—check for need for replacement /___Check roller furling gear for smooth operation and need for lubrication /___Check extrusion section joint areas over the forestay for abrasion and wear/___Lube as needed, per owner's manual/___Halyards—check condition and replace or swap end for end

Engine

Inboard:___Check engine oil (should have been changed in fall layup)/___ Check below engine for oil or water leaks /___Check for loose nuts, rust or discoloration / ___Replace spark or glow plugs /___Replace filters or filter elements including fuel line filter and air filter /___Double check all fuel lines for condition, chafe, and for tightness of clamps / ___Check transmission oil and gear case lubricant / ___Check raw water intake strainers. Also check inlet /___ Check pump impeller, hoses, hose clamps. Replace any soft hoses or rusted clamps /___Check belts for condition and tension—replace as necessary / ___ Check antisiphon valve fitting, if your sailboat has one / ___Check engine block drains/___freeze plugs for discoloration or leaks / ___Check your supply of spare engine equipment and parts. Can you make basic emergency repairs / ___Check and clean backfire flame arrestor /___Add fresh fuel /___Check fuel shut-off and tank valves / ___Test fume detector and blower fan/ ____Check owner's manual for additional inspections/

Outboard: Replace plugs if you did not do so in your fall layup / ___Spark plug boots on securely and in good condition/___Check spark plug wires condition to be certain they are not cracked, abraded or deteriorated /___Check prop—if bent, chipped or worn replace or take it to a prop shop for work /___Check gear lube (it should be full and have been changed in your fall layup) /___Check engine for leaks, discolorations, worn parts, loose nuts /___Inspect fuel line fittings for tight fit, cleanliness, evidence of leaks / Check fuel tank and hoses/ ___Replace hose or bulb primer if soft or looks abraded /___Check and replace anodes as needed /___Clean and oil throttle parts; lube shift mechanism and other moving items for smoothness /___Touch up paint /___Clean engine inside and out; look over for general condition. /___Drain fuel tank and fuel line of old gas, if you have not done so already. Fill with fresh gas and oil mix (if required)

Electrical

___**Check the condition** of the batteries, including need for recharging/___ Check terminal connections for tightness and connection /___Check water level (if you have that type of battery) / ___Check wiring for loose connections, chafe, etc./ ___Check all systems/ bulbs to see that they function / ___Battery is securely mounted ___Check VHF radio, other electronic gear to be certain they function properly.

Safety

___Check availability** and condition of all safety items including:___PFD's (enough for all people who will be on board) /___Whistles /___Flashlights (do they work OK Extra batteries & bulbs) /___Man-overboard throwable and line /___Distress flares /___Fire extinguisher (check pressure) /___radar reflector /___Soft wood tapered plugs beside through-hulls for emergency use; extras for emergency holing /___Space blanket /___First aid kit with adequate supplies / ___Emergency tools including duct tape, underwater epoxy, repair items for hull, sail repair kit, heavy wire cutters, extra shackles, clamps, etc. for repair of rigging, and emergency tiller

Sails

___**Inspect sails** for overall condition /___Check areas of stress needing sailmaker's attention such as threads loosening /___Check pockets, battens / ___Check need for cleaning and or replacement/ ___Send to sailmakers for upgrade/ recutting

Trailer

___**Double check** tire pressures /___Check condition of grease in bearings; add waterproof grease /___Check wheel bearings for wear and pitting as recommended/___Check pressurized bearing protection for leaks /___Check bearing grease seals for leaks /___Check trailer for rust—touch up with rust-inhibiting primer & paint / ___Clean and oil winch /___Check condition of rope or cable / ___Lights and electricals functioning/ ___Double check brakes and hydraulic fluid /___Be certain all bolts and nuts are tight and that all supports are correct to support the boat /___License is current

General

___**Check** that your on-board personal gear is in order, including ___sunglasses ____cap with visor____nylon jacket ___safety harness____foul weather gear, including suit and deckboots ____sunblocker_____ointments ____insect repellent /___determine that your boat's registration and license are current

Spring Action schedule

My spring commissioning list:

Work to be completed as compiled from my Spring commissioning checklist inspections

Item   **Work to be completed**

Fall Layup

Checklist for fall layup and storage

Check spring list for general inspection. Plus additionally check the following:

Hull

___**Check hull** for overall condition and cleaning. Look for nicks, abrasions, scrapes, etc. /___Clean and polish hull/___Note condition of antifouling (order for spring replacement) /___Condition and location of osmotic blisters (let hull dry out and fill next spring) /___Check rudder & condition of fittings, in particular, for signs of excess play. Check rudder packing gland (order new fittings for spring)/ ___Drains are clear/___Check propeller for nicks, bent blades—send to prop shop /___On prop, check security of lock nut and that its safety wire or pin are secure and not worn/___For inboard engine, check shaft strut, cutlass bearing for excessive play. Check stuffing box for signs of leaks/ ___Check zincs for condition and need for replacement. If a zinc is on shaft, see if it is not deteriorated and loose.

Topsides

___**Gelcoat** cracks, crazing or delamination/___ Stress or other fiberglass cracks /___ Need for refinishing: have hull repainted /___Hatches & hatch seals Ok—no leaks during season

Belowdecks

___**Check** cabinets, storage areas for removal of food items and other items which may freeze or which should be removed prior to boat storage/ ___Check bilges for dryness and cleanliness/ ___Check area around chainplates for stress cracks or delamination. If chainplate is bolted to bulkhead, check bulkhead-to-hull glassed in area for cracks or delamination or signs that this is "working"/ ___Check keelboats for condition and tightness/

Equipment topsides

___**Ground** tackle condition and cleanliness. Check anchor shackles for wear. Check also safety wire holding shackle pin closed/ ___Winches—need for cleaning and greasing /___Cockpit drains—open /___Lines—need taking off boat, cleaning, or replacement for next season/ ___Check compasses for condition, loss of fluid

Mast & rigging

___Overall condition** of mast & sail track /___Rivets or screws are solid and have no rust or corrosion/___Clean sail track /___Turnbuckles—bent turnbuckles or worn threads/___Rigging—check stainless wires for smoothness (no fishhooks) / ___Check end fittings for stress—broken strands, discoloration, or signs of coming apart of bulging /___Check to see that mast, if out of boat, is supported and carefully stored / ___Masthead fittings and sheaves—check for looseness, corrosion, fatigue/ __Check also that the halyards, where they pass through the sheaves, are in good condition. __Swap end for end __ Replace

Engine

Inboard/ ___Drain fuel from engine and other storage procedure recommended by owner's manual /___Check below engine for oil or water leaks / ___Replace engine oil / ___Replace spark plugs/ ___Check for loose nuts, items, rust or discolorations /___Check and clean or replace filters including fuel line filter and air filter /___Double check all fuel lines for condition, chafe, and for tightness of clamps/___Change transmission oil /___On outboards/ or inboard-outboard drive units, replace gear case lubricant /___Check raw water intake strainers / ___Check seacocks, inlets/ ___Check pump impeller, hoses, hose clamps /___Drain coolant / ___ Check pulleys for condition and tension—replace as necessary /___Check antisiphon valve fitting, if boat has one /___Check engine block drains/ freeze plugs for discoloration or leaks /___If recommended, add non-alcohol water absorbative or fuel conditioner to fuel tank / ___Check over ship's supply of spare parts and order for engine for next season, including plugs, points, filters, belts, impellers, hoses/ ___Check with other owners to determine what problems they have encountered so that you can order "spares" for emergency use when you need them (Add to **Purchasing Organizer & Record**, page 26)

Outboard: ___Remove old fuel from system, including gas line, engine and gas tank / ___Replace plugs /___Check prop---if bent, chipped or worn replace or take it to a prop shop for work /___Change gear lube, oil/ ___Check engine over for leaks, discolorations, worn parts, loose nuts/___Inspect fuel line fittings for tight fit, cleanliness, no evidence of leaks /___Check fuel tank and hoses. Replace hose or bulb primer if soft or abraded /___Anodes OK/

Electrical

__**Check** the condition of the batteries, including need for recharging, terminal connections, water level (if you have that type of battery) /___Check fluid level if your battery requires this / ___Check all systems/ bulbs to see determine repairs and replacements for next season/ ___Check equipment lighting, such as compass.

Fall action schedule

My Fall layup list: Items to be completed as compiled from my fall layup checklist inspections

Item	Description of work

Section 6

Emergency

Captain's emergency instructions

Man overboard

VHF radio emergency calls

Fire

Hull taking on water

Emergency instructions

Man overboard

In a man-overboard situation, the crew should be well rehearsed to handle any accident. Generally speaking, most man-overboard procedures consist of the following steps: **1/** One crew member keeps his/ her eyes always on the person overboard and points to the victim continuously **2/** A man-overboard throwable float or life preserver is thrown to victim **3/** The helmsman turns the boat around **4/** The boat approaches the victim and carefully comes near **5/** The victim is aided on board

The **captain's orders** for a man overboard drill and emergency are as follows:

....

....

....

....

....

....

....

....

Man overboard throwable and gear are located as indicated:

Dates of "man-overboard" drills:

VHF radio emergency calls

The VHF radio is the main way to get help afloat. All members of the crew should be able to operate it and be drilled on its use for an **emergency**. To use the VHF radio during an emergency, the general procedures are: **1/** Turn on VHF Radio, volume on high **2/** Select Channel 16 **3/** Depress transmit button on mike and repeat the words, "**Pan**," three times (do not say *Mayday* unless you are in grave and imminent danger, such as immediate sinking) **4/** Say your call station, name of your vessel, and that you are trying to make contact with anyone listening. Example: "*Pan, Pan, Pan.* This is the sailboat *Intrepid*. I will talk to anyone listening. Over." **5/** Repeat this twice, then release the transmit button and listen to the response. **6/** After another station contacts you, you will go to another channel. Respond by pressing the button, then repeating the instruction, such as "This is *Intrepid*. I am going to Channel __. Over." **7/** Switch to the designated channel and communicate by repeating the name of the caller, your name, and your distress message. **Example:** "Sailboat *Nightwind*, this is sailboat *Intrepid*. (Say your distress message—the nature of your problem). Do you read? Over." **8/** When you are finished, repeat the name of your sailboat and say, "This is (name), call letters, and Out."

Our Call Letters:_____

The captain's orders to make an emergency call on the ship's VHF radio

....

....

....

....

....

....

Mayday message--highest priority, boat is sinking. A *Mayday* message has the following steps: 1/ The vessel in distress transmits *Mayday*, three times 2/ This is followed by the vessel's call station and name three times. 3/ Next, your location to known bearings, if near shore, or longitude and latitude if at sea 4/ Next, the vessel's problem and kind of assistance required 5/ Time permitting, the vessel should transmit other information which might help the rescuer, such as the boat type, colors, length, make, plus number of persons onboard, or other special information.

Example: *"Mayday, Mayday, Mayday.* This is_____ (give call letters), the sailboat *Yeller, Yeller, Yeller.* I am an estimated 8 miles offshore on a bearing directly west of Cornucopia harbor. We have hit submerged object, are holed and sinking. Our course is east directly toward the harbor entrance, speed is 2 knots. Pumps are on and we estimate our time afloat is less than one hour. We request vessel with extra pumps to assistant and to standby. *Yeller* is 30-foot yellow sailboat with yellow sails and four persons aboard. We are sinking. *Mayday, Mayday, Mayday."* After repeating this three times, say "Over," and listen for a responding vessel.

The VHF radio, call letters, and additional instructions are located here:

Dates crew rehearsed on VHF radio emergency procedures:

Fire

The first tool to use to fight most shipboard fires is the fire extinguisher. Each crew member should know the exact location of each fire extinguisher, its type (such as Type A, B, or C) and be drilled in its specific application,

The vessel has on board the following types of fire extinguishers for use on these **types of fires:**

Extinguisher Type	**For use on these fires onboard**
1/ _____	_____
2/ _____	_____
3/ _____	_____
4/ _____	_____

Captain's special instructions:

Location of fire extinguisher(s) on vessel:

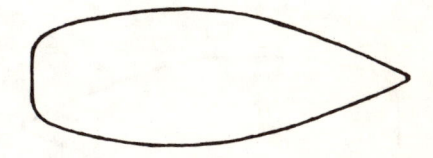

Dates crew drilled on fire emergency and use of extinguisher:

Hull taking on water

When the boat is holed or begins taking on water, the following steps are generally recommended: **1/** Turn on electric pump or pumps **2/** Inspect for damage **3/** Stuff materials into hole to stop the water coming in or lessen the inflow. Anything will help, including clothing, bedding, sails; however, if the hole is small, a special round tapered plug of soft wood can be hammered through. For a larger hole, mattresses, slats, table leaves, or anything wooden can be jammed or pressured in place. In some cases, an extra sail or nylon tarp can be slung over the outside of the hull and worked to the area of the hole, helping stem the leak.

Captain's Procedures:

List of Emergency holing supplies kept on board:

Location of emergency holing supplies:

Bilge pump locations:

Extra pans, buckets, for bucket brigade:

Section 7

Records, Systems & Costs

Galley basics

Boat supplies

Chart locker

Rope locker

Names, addresses & telephone numbers

Expenditures Record

Appointments & schedules

Galley basics

This is a list of **basic supplies** in your galley. Note which need to be replaced during your next shopping trip and date of resupply. Also, here is where you can keep track of new provisioning for your next short cruise. You can use **Galley basics** as your "shopping list" for your galley.

Current basic supplies   Resupply

New Provisions

Boat supplies

Here is a list of basic supplies for your boat. Write down items as you think of them or as they need to be replaced

Chart locker

Keep a record of the charts and maps you have on hand. At the left, note the official number of the chart, then list the "name of the chart" and at right, the date of its issuance, any notes you have, such as when you last used it and any special observations. On the next page, add those charts you want to order for future cruises or to replace current charts.

Chart #	Name of Chart	Date	Notes

Reminder to order new charts:

Rope locker

Itemize the lines you have on board, their current location, size and the date they began service so that you can rotate and replace them to minimize breakage and problems.

Line use	Material	Diameter	Length	Date Put in Use

Order new lines as follows:

Boat gear locator

Here you can make a list of the extra gear you carry on board and its location. For example, if you have a pump repair kit, located under the cabin sole near your current pump, you can list that for easy reference.

Gear item	Description	Location

Names & addresses

People you want to maintain contact with: Names, telephone number (including area code), and mailing addresses. It's useful to write the circumstances, also, in Notes, such as "skippers of sloop, *Tralee,* met at Windjammer festival in Boston on July 12.. Great folks!"

Name   Telephone

Address   City   State,   Zip

Notes

Name   Telephone

Address   City   State,   Zip

Notes

Name   Telephone

Address   City   State,   Zip

Notes

Name	Telephone
Address	City	State,	Zip

Notes

Name	Telephone
Address	City	State,	Zip

Notes

Name	Telephone
Address	City	State,	Zip

Notes

Name	Telephone
Address	City	State,	Zip

Notes

Expenditures

Costs incurred for your vessel and its operation. This can include slip fee, insurance costs, fuel, routine maintenance, supplies, replacement of equipment, new gear and equipment, etc.

Year

Date	Item	Cost

Total:

Year:

Date	Item	Cost

Total

$ $ $ $ $ $ $

Appointments & schedules

Your specific **appointments** and **schedules** for your boat. This can range from the time of your next haul out, or when your marina slip fee comes due, to the dates you are taking guests out for a pleasure cruise.

Name of appointment or item	**Description**	**Time**	**Date**

Name of appointment or item   **Description**   **Time**   **Date**

Name of appointment or item	**Description**	**Time**	**Date**

Comments on the Boat Book? Want to share an idea? We'd like to hear your thoughts and suggestions. Write to the Editor, **MarLor's BOAT BOOK**, 4304 Brigadoon Dr., St. Paul, MN. 55126. *Thank you.*